THIS UNCERTAIN VOYAGE

Susan Dworski Nusbaum

coffeetownpress
Kenmore, WA

coffeetownpress

A Coffeetown Press book published by Epicenter Press

Epicenter Press
6524 NE 181st St.
Suite 2
Kenmore, WA 98028

For more information go to:
www.Camelpress.com
www.Coffeetownpress.com
www.Epicenterpress.com
www.SusanDworskiNusbaum.com

All rights reserved. No part of this book may be reproduced or transmitted in any form or by any means, electronic or mechanical, including photocopying, recording, or any information storage and retrieval system, without permission in writing from the publisher.

This is a work of fiction. Names, characters, places, brands, media, and incidents are either the product of the author's imagination or are used fictitiously.

Cover image: "Big Sky" by Susan Copley

This Uncertain Voyage
Copyright © 2024 by Susan Dworski Nusbaum

Library of Congress Control Number: 2023945711

ISBN: 978-1-68492-141-6 (Trade Paper)
ISBN: 978-1-68492-142-3 (eBook)

For Jane, Tom, and Peter

Acknowledgements

These poems have appeared or will appear
in the following publications:

Haggadah: *Connecticut River Review*

Sarabande: *Chautauqua Review*

Alleluia: *The Buffalo News*

Distancing: *The Buffalo News*

Contents

I . . . beheld but not held

Dragonflies 3
Flash Drive 5
Pipes and Timbrels 7
Gallery 9
Kinderszenen
    Backyard 11
    Born Yesterday 13
    Inheritance 15
Bells 17
Sarabande 19
The Substitute 21
Hotel 23
Driving Away 25

II . . . around the bend

Riverbend 29
Tall Clock 31
Hush 33
Scab 35
Breaking 37
Bending 39
The Spaciousness of Dark 41
Hunger 43
Birthday 45
These Foolish Things 47
All Hallows' Eve 49
Avatar 51
Thunder 53
Distancing 55
Passover Zoom 57

Chalk Work 59
Anti-Silence 61
Heart 63

III . . . breathing
Breathing 67
Lady Liberty 69
Haggadah 71
Atonement 73
Replacement Theory 75
Ballot 77

IV . . . this accidental habitat
The Wonder 81
Tropical Sunrise 83
Watching for Manatees 85
Intelligent Design 87
The Elephant Speaks of Love 89
Burn 91
Pause 93
Messages 95
Black Ice 97
Yigdal 99
Alleluia 101
Traces 103
Saturday Farmers' Market 105
The Short Life of the Magnolia 107
Summer Day 109

I.

. . . beheld but not held

Dragonflies
After a photograph, "Crane Flies Mating as June Bug Looks On,"
by Mary Jane Nusbaum

Two slender dragonflies
rest lightly on the outside of a screen,
mirrored end to end,
transparencies of wings
scored by wire-mesh squares,

natural grace
visible but untouchable—
this remoteness, what is, what was,
beheld but not held, sifted images
floating on mesh, on lens, on cornea.

Look again. This time, read the title. No,
not dragonflies, but common crane flies,
not passively juxtaposed, but mating,
their final act before dying,
wings flared, filament-limbs outstretched,
silent, for all I know.

A fat June bug, mesh-embroidered,
has a clear view from one corner,
absorbing every rustle, every quiver.

Flash Drive
for Jane

The flash-drive you sent me opened my life.

Here you are, my daughter, radiant
in a prom dress, gardenia at your wrist.
There's your brother, capped and gowned,
another brother, helmeted on the backyard rink,
hockey stick in hand.

And snapshots of Dad in an apron,
carving the Thanksgiving turkey,
and me, mini-skirted
in front of that flocked wallpaper,
all the rage,

eating lobster at the Cape,
faces shiny with butter,
riding an elephant
through the pinkness of Jaipur,
holding on for dear life.

Smoldering campfires, Half Dome in the background,
tanned faces to windward, speckled with salt.
Shaggy beards and waxed moustaches,
Mother's fox collar, Daddy's undershirt,
Children hugging, mugging. Friends I've lost.

They touch me in real time, these images.
I can open another era at any hour, and in a flash,
without regret and only a little sadness,
walk my old self through the fullness of my life
and believe in it,

buoyed by the talc-y nuzzle of babies,
conspiratorial glances,
the sexy connection of eyes and bodies,
a timeless love.

And didn't I look good?

Pipes and Timbrels
Ode on a Photograph

Faded tulips, pine branches bleached
through decades propped on a sunny book-shelf—
this over-exposed black and white photo,

portrait of my three small children
girl and two boys planted like flowers
in the backyard garden,

her tousled hair
curling over her shoulder,
lips parted as if to ask a question,

long-lashed boy frowning slightly at the interruption,
fingering a berry just-picked
from the speckled Japonica beside him,

and posing plump in his striped sweater,
the youngest child, knee-deep in pachysandra,
smiling directly into the lens.

No pipes and timbrels here,
only birdsongs, buzz of insects,
a dog barking in the distance.

There you are, my children, captured forever
in your natural habitat like bees in amber,
unconcerned, in this moment,
with the vast world beyond the wooden fence.

You cannot smell the scent of autumn,
or feel the bite of winter, cannot know, as I do,
the unfolding of your lives just beginning to blossom,

believing only in the beauty of the garden,
the miracle of growth, warmth of June sunshine.
This is your truth and all you need to know.

Gallery

Confined by an April snow,
I gaze at artworks on my walls,
reminisce about the times we drove
to New York City with hardly a penny,

rushed to a gallery that sold good art, cheap—
prints of all kinds, woodcuts and etchings,
lithographs by unknown artists, some unsigned,
or old re-strikes by famous ones, like Morisot and LeGros.

We couldn't wait to bring them home,
place them on the drywall of our new house
over the hand-me-down sofa or kitchen table
so we could savor them every day,

spinnaker-ed sailboats, pastorals, colorful abstracts—
some have found new homes with the children
who grew up with them. But the filmy cityscapes,
mothers with children, old opera posters— these hang

on my plaster walls like framed windows flung open
into the heat of young marriage, big-city fever,
into the visions of artists whose names I've forgotten,
enlarging my shuttered life.

Kinderszenen

1. Backyard

As the swing arcs
toward a sliver of day-moon,
new shoes scuff
patches of dirt, fingers
clutch rusty chain links,
face tilted sunward.

On every side,
an intoxication—
clouds of purple lilacs,
bees gathering on yellow roses,
a glimpse of violets
in the shadow of a fence.

Behind the back porch
a scraggly victory garden
waits for harvest,
radishes and carrots
nestled in dirt, warm tomatoes
split by thirsty starlings.

Distant rasps of a rake
mingle with scrambled
kitchen clatter, radio chatter.
Patty practices the piano,
snatches of Schumann
escaping through the screen door.

And standing by the steps,
a full-throated soprano
lengthens the syllables of my name,
calling me in.

2. Born Yesterday

Every wintery Saturday,
safe from the tramp of goosesteps "over there,"
my sister and I would read plays aloud
from a collection our mother got
from the Book-of-the-Month Club,
Best American Plays, 1940 to 1945.
Those were the years Our Boys
marched off and came back—
or didn't.

Snug under an Afghan on the studio-couch,
we divvied up parts—I, the younger,
got butler or third bystander, my sister
helping me with the hard words.

She inhabited the important roles—
timid Laura in *The Glass Menagerie,*
the evil Count in *Watch on the Rhine,*
Our Town's Emily.

Oblivious, we breezed
through scene after scene,
stories about frustration and lost dreams,
betrayal and suicide,
hunger and war,

sniggering at words we didn't understand
but knew were off-limits,
like "gigolo" and "slut,"
and "Gestapo,"
pausing for a moment when

Emily suddenly cries from her grave,

> *I never realized before*
> *how troubled and how in the dark*
> *live persons are . . . It goes so fast.*
> *We don't have time to look at one another . . .*

3. Inheritance

My mother's table,
small, marble-topped,
found a new home

beside my wing chair
in one corner of the living room,

still wobbly, loosened
during my childhood
by a long history of its use,

weighed down by stacks
of story books and novels,
Majolica ashtray, an occasional

philodendron, the assemblage
so heavy its feet wore grooves
in mother's green wall-to-wall.

My inheritance—a cushiony lap,
blue-veined hands turning pages,

as vibrations of Schumann,
scent of Estee, swoosh of slip
against stockings, settle around it.

This magnetic field,
an irrevocable trust.
I'm heir to the air.

Bells

After she left,
her scent lingered, settled
on books and upholstery,
perfumed beads, lilac or gardenia,
suspended in air, mixed
with lemon furniture polish,
a hint of yeast.

Who would she be without it—
wrists moistened by wands
from amber vials, purse
redolent of lipstick,
mint candies for concerts,
inhaling as she buries her face
in a child's clutch of lilies-of-the-valley
from the back yard?

What's more truthful
than the floral of her hair,
stiff with spray against my cheek,
or her Ponds-softened skin
the last time I kissed her goodbye?

And what returns her to me?
A trace of Chanel,
line-dried laundry,
a tumbler of white bells
shimmering on my sill.

Sarabande
Bach Cello Suite #4

The music would have been enough.

But this time as I watch
YoYo Ma's performance

I can see

how movement and sound
    meet in the act of music
        spiraling across centuries
            from the cello's hollow
                intimate yet restrained
                    in poised formality
                vibrations shivering
            through fingers
        into the body
    choreography
        of shoulders
            drooping
                on beat two of three
                    the long caress of bow
                nod to fingerboard
            at the end of a phrase
        dissonance
    a furrowed brow
resolution
    a quivering
        head lowered
    And I can see

Bach and Ma joined in dance
fingertips touching
eyes locked.

The Substitute

As she walks on stage,
we rise in appreciation.
Diminutive, plain-faced, sturdy,
called at the last minute to step in
for the famous pianist, suddenly ill—
Rachmaninoff's Second,
so difficult, so dangerously sentimental.

We attend out of curiosity,
sit nervously at the edge of our seats
uplifted by the first chords, stunning crescendo,
promise of rapture to come.
She's strangely familiar—this replacement,
the understudy facing her big chance.

Who hasn't watched from the wings,
or prayed to be chosen
from lists of candidates. Who hasn't wept,
anonymous by the hearth
longing for an invitation to the ball?

At the end of the performance,
the audience leaps up again,
screaming bravos for her fairy-tale success,
the auspicious convergence of skill and luck.
Before playing the encore, she confesses:

> *Just hours ago, I thought I'd be sitting*
> *at home tonight, eating Chinese take-out.*

Hotel

"Home away from home,"
says the brochure.
So orderly, so cool.

I throw my suitcase on the bed,
sink into a wing chair,
glance at walls hung
with photos of pastel hydrangeas,
hang my clothes in a roomy closet
where a white one-size-fits-all bathrobe
waits for me after my shower.

    How delightful
    that someone else
    will clean this bathroom,
    change these sheets,
    that the bed will be turned down
    by invisible hands, a mint poised
    on the crisp pillowcase.

        Nothing here belongs to me,
        no family photos
        to remind me of old times,
        no inherited furniture
        to conjure the faces of dead parents,

        no neighbors ringing my doorbell
        for a little olive oil and conversation,

no decisions to make—
should I re-upholster the couch?
paint the dining room ceiling?

There's no clutter,
nothing to trip over,
nothing to cry over.

A week away in a warm climate.
Only 144 more hours to go.

Driving Away: Five Variations

1.

She raps her knuckles on the Jeep window,
shred of sari across her face.
A corner droops—nose scarred, half-gone.
Abul cranks open a window,
shoves her shoulder from the door.
The Delhi heat, smell of kerosene, rush in.
She squats in dirt, retrieves the coins we toss.
My vision blurs. We pull away. Cinder in my eye.

2.

Mother stands on the porch wrapped in a sweater,
shrinks in the frosted windshield, hand raised
to wave, dab her eyes with a shred of tissue.
Her face blurs as I back away, inching
around snow-mounds, hoping she'll remember
to take her meds, hoping my long-distance
calls will be enough to hold her.
I turn, fasten my seatbelt, flick on the radio.

3.

From her recliner, she pulls me down
to kiss goodbye. "My daughter-in-law,"
she intones, waves the aide to continue dusting.
Wrapped in turquoise fleece, enamel butterfly
fastened in white hair. she complains about
table-mates deaf beyond conversation. The smell
of banana browning in her over-heated room
clings to my sweater, the car seat. I open the windows.

4.

The Tercel inches down La Cienega around fresh scars,
black ashes from chimneys half-gone, LA freeway in shreds.
My son finds a route to LAX through streets
where dazed crowds clump at curbs, heads bowed
over mounds of stones, crumpled bones of houses,
trees wedged into the hoods of cars.
At the terminal, I quake, steady myself to leave him,
wave him into the after-shock of his first disaster alone.

5.

The last shovel of dirt tossed years ago
on a husband's grave, the last stone on stone,
my bowed head finally lifted. Dazed mourners
huddle around a new mound. I pity their half-life,
resolve to leave an over-watered grief worn to shreds.
I sprint across a fresh-mown lawn to the car,
wipe grass from my shoes. Shrinking in the rear-view,
his black marble headstone—cinder in my eye.

II.

. . . around the bend

II.

Around the Sun

Riverbend
(Ceylon, 1970)

From the shelter of the veranda,
my husband and I loved to watch
the Mahaveli Ganga meander toward the Bay of Bengal,
as a parade of elephants and mahouts
grazed halfway up the winding path
to the hilltop bungalow, our paradise for a year.

Lunch over, the mahouts
hitched up their sarongs, seduced
the animals into the river for their daily bath,
murmuring Singhalese words unknown to us,
but understood by elephants,

who willingly obliged, lowering themselves
into the shallows, trusting their caretakers
to scrub their thick hides with coconut shells
as they whispered love poems into their ears.

And we watched the river flow around them in ripples,
tranquil as the course our young lives had taken.

One rainy morning, bursts of gunfire
from across the water shook us awake,
our neighbor Abdul shouting from the road,
"There's a bad war coming, my friends.
Look, look in the river."

Through the downpour, we could make out
two headless human bodies tumbling by,
an indifferent Mahaveli Ganga
sweeping them against the rocks
toward the river's divergence,
muddy whorls obstructing our view.

We grieved, bodies encircled, hands stroking hair,
trusting our bond to keep us afloat, believing
we were protected from the unimaginable,
the truth lying just around the bend.

Tall Clock
for Sandy

Between chemo treatments,
he'd retreat to his garage workshop,
hunching over the tattered plans
to create a beautiful tower as tall as he was,
working non-stop to beat the deadline.

He sanded and oiled the rosewood,
cut grooves for the ebony trim,
formed joints, mortises and tenons, fastened
the curly-maple face, copper numbers and hands,

constructed a sliding walnut panel big enough
to accommodate his wide knuckles
for setting the works, enabling the chimes.

After he hauled the frame upstairs,
he placed it so the copper might catch
a sliver of northern light,
adjusted the movement, wound it on Sundays.

During the darkest hours,
the chimes stirred us, reassurance
that the world was still turning.

Friend who attends my lonely silence,
now you rest unwound, chimes muffled,
your hands and face motionless,
but shining.

Hush

On the morning of your death
as the moon began to disappear,
I was startled awake
not by the rush of departure,
but by a hush, a whisper of consonants,
as if a *fermata* had stopped
the flow of time, marking
the end of a symphonic passage,
its birds-eye widening
to recapture sonorities
lost in the stillness.

No doubt some sounds
lingered that morning—
whir of the ceiling fan,
water hissing in pipes
inside the thick walls
of our house.
Surely branches scratched
against our bedroom window,
and doves spilled their vowels
into the empty air.

I could not hear the dawn
because your voice
was missing.

And the day broke without you.

Scab

Sudden seepage
staining
the membrane
around my heart

an old deception
never quite healed

the ache hanging
around in the chest

a twinge   a cramp
remains of a break

nerve endings
dulled to throb

a slight tear
in the cartilage
invisible now
scarred over

but glistening
in a certain light
in dreams—
abandoned at sea
or buried alive—

and in photos—
Where was I then?
Or you? What
were you thinking?

What did I know?

Breaking

If I'd never known passion for a husband,

if I'd never reached to hold my mother's hand
or bent to hear my child's song,

then gratitude for this diminished world
would be easier to find,

my heart still intact instead of
broken into a hundred sharp pieces,

which scrape against the bones of my chest
in search of wholeness,

as now I strain to recapture—

in the heat of sand, the perfume
of cedar, of candle-wax,

in the promise of thin green blades
breaking through snow—

the flutter of what once nested there.

Bending

From my Adirondack chair
I watch tall grasses dance at the woods' edge.
honey locusts bow in the wind, unbroken,

colorful arcs trace the paths
of finches and jays, as they soar
from feeder to nest,

and nodding on their supple stems,
daylilies turn their faces into the sun.

You, my new husband,
appear at the screen door of our cottage,
holding it open with your elbow,
fingers curled around the handles
of a two warm mugs.
You bend to kiss me.

How miraculous—
that we have changed course intact,
leaning into each other
as we grow toward the morning light,
bending to stay alive.

The Spaciousness of Dark

It's easy to feel crowded when daylight reveals
stains on the upholstery, piles of unfinished papers,
flowers in need of tossing, shrinking days crammed
with diversions, tasks requiring attention.

But in the night-dark   every shadow   every sound
                        a dim presence

trees dissolve   limbs silenced   birds flown
              a nightstand   with its book and lamp   floats
      on sea of black   each   passing   car   loses
direction   sirens   doppler   to pianissimo

Released into the vast living-room of memory
I hear the faint   ring of a telephone   evaporating
       somewhere   inside a building
or on a sidewalk

Could that be you sending me signals
       hovering at the edge of my dreams
              ready to keep me company?

Come in, my love, I've cleared a space for you

    There's plenty of room

    inside this darkness.

Hunger

A steamy plate
of polenta and shrimp ragout,
night redolent with the spice of skin
sifting into downy comfort,
fullness of shoulder
tucked beneath shoulder,
thigh on thigh, arms askew.

It's easy to forget for a moment,
the hump of pillows piled across the bed.
Bit by bit, memory returns;
bit by bit, longing seeps
into the ragged texture of dreams—

ripples of appetite
lap at the edge of absence—
the taste of Brunello, spill of corn meal,
tomato paste dried on the counter,
the lingering sea-smell
of crustaceans cracked and peeled and eaten—

no sensation sharp enough
to break the fast.
Hunger feasts on remembering.

Birthday
for Ron

For eleven years on September 1st
I memorialized your death with a candle,
but today I had to check your obituary
to find the date of your birth,
August 26th—
information lost somehow
inside a blank space in my brain.

But I remember every one
of those final days—you
insisting we drive to Chautauqua,
to meet one more time
with our Wednesday gathering of friends,
your labored breathing as you slept in the car,
reassuring me you were still alive.

On the deck overlooking the lake
a glorious birthday party—
Mary Anne and Georgia vying to sit beside you,
Bob on the glider, toasting you with his usual Martini,
Rodney and Gina serving you from the buffet counter,
plates piled with lasagna and bean salad,
John providing not one, but two tall birthday cakes.

And the next day back home,
a celebration at the new Burmese restaurant
with Madeline and David and their family,
pre-ordered specialties of the house—
Mango chicken and black rice papaya salad,
spicy noodles, Kat Kyay Kote.

Then another home-baked cake
and a raucous rendition of "Happy Birthday"
as you blew out the flames of your years,
the gleaming embers lingering on tiny wicks
long after your breath had stopped.

These Foolish Things
(*homage to Ella*)

It's not the bottle of Wine-Away in the cupboard,
or the pink stain on the white carpet,

not the glass beads you bought me in Murano,
or the silly grin you wore in our wedding photos.

not the yellow orchid I bought you as you were dying,
or your driver's license saved in my top drawer.

It's the warm breath from the bedroom window stirring my hair.

Oh, how your arms cling around my shoulders,
ghostly whispers in my ear. *And still*

my heart has wings.

All Hallows' Eve

In the butterscotch light of late October,
they appear wherever I walk—
Ferry St, the stone mansion at the corner,
Sandy waving as he sails
from the chimney of his first office,

past Al and Diane, still clinking martinis
on the steps to their boarded-up second floor flat,
lawn wild with weeds,
their golden retriever haunting
the front bushes, sniffing for treats.

Right turn on Tudor, where inside
Ansie's old house, shades of past lives
float down the curved staircase to breakfast,
and the neighbor-woman dances
among the hollyhocks in her garden.

The rustle under my sneakers
conjures the spirit of my father,
tattered hat hiding his baldness,
rasp of his rake against leaves
which never stop falling,

my sister and I burying each other
in mold-fragrant piles at the curb,
Mother materializing on the front porch
in apron and high heels
to scold about the mess.

Soon the kisses and candy-corn will be
given and gone. In the deepening darkness,
I'll summon up my cadre of ghosts,
trusting them, as I always do,
to quicken my heart, remind me I'm alive.

Avatar

A solitary morning walker
sun low at his back
hunched into his hoodie
against the April wind
walks briskly almost runs
then stops cold.

Thought he was alone
but looming ahead
his shadow
elongated   featureless
swinging limbs
translucent
webbed with cracks
hyacinth and myrtle
paled along the curb.

One at a time
he raises an arm
watches his shade
overtake porches
slide over chimneys
measures the sweep
of his movements
his shape now shrinking
in the rising sun
as it fills his boots.

Begins to move
footsteps quickening
face lifted
toward the sun's light
now overhead
feels its warmth
the weight of days
at his back
a dark companion
around his shoulders.

Thunder

Mrs. Edmonds sold corsets
at my father's store,

discreetly measured
each dimpled thigh,
matronly overhang,

to assure a perfectly
supported torso,

her own figure slim,
shapely in a pastel-blue suit,
her rust-grey perm
secured with a bobby pin.

On Saturday afternoons
she fed me red licorice

while I read comic books
and modeled ladies' hats
before the 3-way mirror,

and every Christmas Eve
she appeared at our house
with her only child Keith

to deliver a fruitcake
baked in a Maxwell House tin.

One day she called my father
to say she wouldn't be in.

Lightning had struck
and killed her Keith
as he was picking cherries
from their tree.

Mrs. E turned ashen, lumpy,
her hair thinned and hung unpinned,

her breath smelled overripe,
like Juicy Fruit and cigarettes.

Soon no one wore corsets anymore,
and she flickered away.

I never knew her first name.

Even now, when lightning rips
the summer sky,

I count down the seconds
until the clap of thunder,

picture a boy sprawled
jagged on the grass,

blood-bright spill of cherries
across the lawn,

odors of ozone and red licorice
hanging in air.

Distancing

This virus invades lungs
through lips and nostrils,
wherever a hand touches
a knob, a railing, a cup,
in a sneeze, a cough, a laugh,
        a kiss.

In this world, already fractured,
I move farther away
to avoid contagion, chat
in prolonged phone conversations,
        long distance or not at all,

learn to find what I love
hidden away in cupboards
as I clean house—
        a shawl from Italy,
        a silver heart on a chain,
        a missing button.

Now I take walks alone,
part of a familiar landscape,

        a chorus of March birds—
        cardinals, robins, woodpeckers
        hiding in waking elms,

            locust pods
            rattling in the wind
            waiting to burst,

shoots of crocus
lifting themselves through the mud,
where snow once blanketed a garden.

And just this morning,
those two rows of horse-chestnut trees
have burst into rosy torches,
gladdening both sides of Bryant Street.

My extended family miraculously enlarged!

Passover Zoom
April 2020

Tonight I tune in
to a family Passover seder,
this year on my IPad,
and remember how this night
is different from all other nights,
and how our people escaped tyranny
and a host of plagues
by trekking through the desert
for 40 years, no end in sight.

We arrive in little squares on a screen,
portraits of the people I love,
who interrupt each other trying to get a word in,
voices sometimes electronically garbled,
but cherishing the view more than the words,
each one enduring a common desert trek,
thirsting for the comfort of touch,
the safety of closeness,
a return to a life in which
tomorrow might unfold into eternity,
and uncertainty, shrink to nothing.

We're reminded of Spring,
our plates filled with the greens of rebirth,
we taste the bitter tears of suffering,
the sweet fruit of hard work,
singing of gratitude
for the sufficiency of our lives,
even in the face of hardship.
Dayenu. It would be enough.

As the story ends,
Elijah appears at our doors.
And we let him in.

Chalk Work

Scribbled on the sidewalk
in large pastel letters,
a rainbow arcing below the words,
    BE WELL
gift of a home-bound child,
boredom relieved by distraction,

and the pleasure of showing kindness
to neighbors and stir-crazy walkers like me,
who search for unfamiliar sidewalks
to explore during the pandemic.

In the pebbled cement beneath the message—
decades of hopscotch grids,
grooves worn smooth by jump-ropers,
portraits of school-mates and pets
drawn by dozens of children long gone,
saved from the tyranny of confinement,

children released in the wash of fresh air,
the heft of fat chalk in their fists,
rainbows coming off on their hands
as they choose their favorite colors
for the crooked lines and block letters,

careful not to smudge with their elbows
this expression of goodwill,
connecting viewer and artist
in an uncertain world.

Anti-Silence

Give me music, give me voice,
give me the whir of washer,
silverware rattling,
give me this wailing wind
pulling me into the light of morning.

I enjoy hearing footsteps
delivering my paper outside the door,
clicking on the news, the hyped-up,
scream-pitched warnings:
viral contagion, racial violence.

Hurray for the recycling truck
rumbling under my window,
receiving yesterday's *New York Times*,
making room for a new day.

Sure, I might like a breather once in a while,
insulate myself from bad news, clanking radiators.
But when my brain needs an auditory nudge,
I rush to the solace of telephone,
Haydn quartet, whistle of kettle,

puree an artichoke soup in the Cuisinart,
sizzle a grilled cheese sandwich
in the cast iron frying pan, warmed
by it's symphony of spatters.

This proclivity's shaped
by my quiet life these recent years—
raucous children, the lovely muddle of arguments,
slap of hockey puck against the garage door.
And in my ear, my name, a whisper—

These are the sounds I grieve for.

Heart
for Mark, my step-son
(April 9, 1962-August 3, 2020)

1.

Miles from here in a Covid-19 unit,
a machine pumps his blood through a tube
and returns it to his body,
limp against the hospital sheets.

Can he see the shadows
scurrying in and out of his room,
sense his dead father stroking his cheek,
his mother beckoning from the grave?

Does he hear the ragged gasps
of the wife at his bedside,
who attends his every breath, the rise
and fall of his chest, or her weeping

as she tosses alone on her bed,
her long marriage lying slack beside her,
who revisits the shining moments of her past,
the empty present glaring back?

And the urgent rhythms inside my chest,
can he feel them launched across the distance,
to penetrate his failing heart,
to quicken it?

2.

Last night the pump went silent.
A family gathers in the house he built,
stripped of a doting father,
an enduring affection,
lives suddenly unplugged,
futures blurred into darkness.

And from afar, I mourn my connection
to a brief but enchanted past,
the fading memories of my heart,
remnants gathered and preserved
in this young man, his only child,
my lost son of my lost husband.

III.

. . . breathing

Breathing

Shouts of protest
in memory of George Floyd
and thousands before him,
whose breathing was stifled
by the knee of hatred,
air squeezed from lungs
by noose and chain and boot,
by the artillery of bigotry
pressed against chests,
to immobilize, dehumanize.

With every free inhalation
I struggle to escape
the strangle-hold of Covid
lurking in the sweet air
as I gasp for each breath.
Yet I suffer from a virulence
more insidious, more suffocating,
my lungs sickened
by complacency,
the knee of complicity
planted firmly
on my trachea.

Lady Liberty

On nice days, she hung the wet wash
on the backyard clothesline
to whiten in the sun,

her right arm raised high, like a sentinel,
clutching a corner of a bedsheet,

her left, reaching down so I could hand her
a wooden clothespin from the bag.

Without halo or torch,
this daughter of the "tempest tost,"
loved her country unconditionally,

belted out "God Bless America,"
right along with Kate Smith.

She was proud her family "made it,"
declined to travel abroad with my father,

insisting, "I'll stay here in the good old USA,
the best country on earth."

Surely she must have read of lynchings
and Japanese detention camps,

knew our own family was unwelcome,
in certain neighborhoods and clubs.

and more than once had been called
a *dirty Jew.*

Today blood stains spread in plain sight across our flag,
massacres commonplace, violence almost expected
in grocery stores, schools, churches and synagogues.

Would my mother bleach them from her mind?
Would she dry them in the sun?

Would she lift her voice in praise?

Haggadah
(The Telling)
for Moshe Dworski

He steadies himself against the starboard rail,
shivers, swallows hard at each slap of wave,
peers across the dark sea into the wake,
Raczki to Bremen—
an oniony kiss,
a calloused hand stroking
the new beard sprouting on his cheek.

This boy Moses, aged 15, traveling alone,
follows the paths of his brothers,
as one by one, they escaped the terror of Cossacks—
clatter of horses, wild through the village,
hoots of drunken marauders,
Mrs. Levitinsky's wailing
at the tiny wooden synagogue's bloody gate,
the flames, the ash.

His fellow passengers do not speak Yiddish.
He fingers his tzitzit each morning,
prays he'll recognize his brother's face at the dock,
longs for an embrace, a table, a plate of soup.

I think of this boy, my grandfather, as I read
about waves of oppressed
Salvadorans, Guatemalans, Hondurans
rolling toward our country, the promised land,
families crashing in exhaustion against our gates,
bodies of their dead—flotsam at the road's edge.

I think of this boy, my grandfather, as I read
about Carlos Gregorio Hernandez Vasquez,
who fled gang violence and certain death in Guatemala
to join his father who came before him,
detained with hundreds of other children
inside a lice-ridden, windowless encampment
in Brownsville TX,

This boy Carlos, aged 16, traveling alone,
shivering with fever,
pronounced dead after weeks of internment.

A newspaper headline records his ending:
Fifth child to die in detention at the border.

Who will tell his story?

Atonement

Every year before Rosh Hashanah,
my grandfather brought home four chickens,
kept them in the basement in wire cages
among jars of dill pickles and metal racks
hung with the double-breasted suits he peddled
to Negroes who'd fled north from lynching-country.

I was eight when first I sensed something alive
huddled by the coal bin, visited them every day,
whined in protest before their final trip to the *schochet*.
gasped when Grandpa hung them limp and dripping
from a clothesline on the back porch.

After I watched Grandma pull their soft quills, singe
the pin feathers until they were naked, gut and salt them,
I skipped across the backyard to collect
the last raspberries of the old year.

When the family gathered to bless the round challah,
I murmured my own blessing for the chickens,
saying a silent prayer of atonement as I ate,
Al Cheyt for the sin of indifference,
in a litany of guilt I'd intone every year from then on.

Replacement Theory
May 14, 2022 (Buffalo NY)

Hugs and hi-fives today
at Tops Friendly Market.
Saturday shoppers weave down aisles
pausing at the deli counter—
what to buy for school lunches,
easy dinners, homework snacks?

What's that? A car backfiring on Jefferson?
Pop-pop. Staccato. Crescendo.

In camouflage and body armor
the shooter has driven 200 miles
to perform his carefully composed attack.

He aims with deadly precision
and shoots.
13 down,
10 dead.
He searches for more.

He knows why he's there,
coached and stoked
by TV racists and demagogues,
a growing army of haters
frenzied by a sinister mission—
*Protect white folks. Eliminate
Blacks and Browns,
Immigrants and Jews.*

We who remain are wounded,
the blood-stained fabric of our home-town
shredding before our eyes.
We mourn the dead, mourn the death
of trust in a just society,
a homeland rich with diversity,
unshakeable until now.

Precisely and with murderous intent,
hatred has ripped through the aisles
of a neighborhood grocery store,
unravelling our dreams of the possible,
replacing them with terror.

Ballot
June 26, 2022

Early-voting
at the Salvation Army.
Here's your ballot, dear,
says the woman at the table.
*Just fill it in over there,
and feed it to the machine
when you're done.*

Outside the trees are dropping
their summer leaves,
the air, stagnant with an ill-wind.
On every corner, a homeless person.
Bullets are flying.

In this morning's News,
I scanned the Court's decision.
War on Women, was the headline.
Bullets are flying.

Catastrophic news
for daughters and granddaughters.
for freedoms in every corner
of this benighted America.
Bullets are flying.

We're dying here, O god of good,
unwilling soldiers in a battle
we failed to see coming.
Can we be saved?
Is anyone still listening?

Here at the Salvation Army,
a machine eats my ballot.
Trees are dropping
their summer leaves.
Bullets are flying

IV.

. . . this accidental habitat

The Wonder

Under the cold December sun, I wonder
what the new James Webb telescope
will teach us, finding stars and galaxies
left over from the Big Bang, 3.8 billion years ago,
the infancy of universes unknown to us.

How implausible is our existence,
hurtling on this speck around
our scattered galaxy, how comforting,
to believe we might learn
the secrets keeping us aloft,

tossed by chance just close enough
and far enough from our Mother Sun
to survive, our ragged cells oozing
with chemicals and fluids,
bouncing among gasses essential
to support our lonely lives.

How incredible, that by finding the past
we might secure our future,
get a second chance, learn
how to protect this earth,
teetering now on the edge of extinction,

simply by examining that confluence
of forces leading to our birth,
leaving for us, lucky trespassers,
a burden we have no choice but to assume—
the rescue of this accidental habitat.

Tropical Sunrise

I exchanged my down parka
for a light blue cardigan,
winter's grey for a limpid sky,
for this view of the sunrise from the lanai,

it's flamboyance deepening and lifting
through the mangroves on the bay,
singeing the horizon, tips of palms, waves
tinged with pomegranate and tangerine,

Every morning I watch
tiny squares of window screen dissolve in sparks
illuminating the landscape—

flocks of crested egrets,
yellow-masked anhinga, dolphins
summoned from their dark grottos,
fishermen, from warm beds—

as a giant kaleidoscope
refracts the new-born day
across a waiting world.

Watching for Manatees

A trace of tropical sun-tan
still colors my skin, now wind-buffeted,
as I return to the Northern dry-cold.

Inside the wintry solitude of home,
war rages in Ukraine, on my screen, in my mind,
its borders violated,

as I search for tranquility
along the shoals of memory,
where immense elliptical shadows glide

beneath the surface, whiskers
parting ripples, bubbles dissolving in air.
Their shapes fade in the shade of a dock,

drift to the far side, disappear into dark
waves of sea-grass, a murky sludge,
emerging in undulating pods.

They do not lose their way, do not sense
the danger of their dwindling habitat
or turn to watch me watching them,

but I can feel their nudge
as we press together
along this uncertain voyage.

Intelligent Design

For 90 minutes inside the Cinema,
Antarctica is home to us,
where emperor penguins, upright and romantic,
play out their harsh lives in march rhythms,
milling around, choosing lovers,

brushing shoulders with neighbors,
feeling who-knows-what about their fate,
as they hold their lives together
with instincts perversely woven
into neural pathways.

Miles away in the August heat,
we wonder what cruel god
would design its brainchildren
for such torment, forcing them to balance
precious eggs on the knuckles of their claws,

protect their species from glacial wind
under belly flaps, and guard their hatchlings
until they grow coats of their own,
until they sense the treacheries
of ice floes and predators.

Who would compel a creature to feel hunger
and the loneliness of abandonment,
or mourn a cracked shell, precious yolk fluid
spilling over ice, to find its only comfort
in the huddled bodies of friends?

What mad scientist would concoct
such a random plan, saving this fragile world
from destruction time and again,
instead of starting over?

The Elephant Speaks of Love
Scientists Confirm Elephant in S. Korea Can Reproduce Speech
Buffalo News

Why are we surprised
to read that another mammal
feels the anguish of isolation
so deeply, he learns to reproduce
his trainer's speech,

that Koshik, the circus performer,
has taught himself the elaborate technique
of placing the tip of his trunk into his mouth
to imitate the frequencies of Korean words,
the sounds his trainer, his only companion, makes?

Separated from his own kind,
he scarcely remembers their comforting
snorts and bellows, slurps and growls.
What creature wouldn't find a way
to greet his only friend?

Koshik knows the power of words
to bring rewards—
nourishment,
whispered endearments,
the attentions of a trainer

who gazes like a grateful lover
into the animal's watery eye,
leans a cheek against his rough haunches,
and caresses his articulate trunk,
spent with language.

Burn

There is no peace here.

Hunched black against blue, the Malibu hills
smolder with waves of weeping, sirens whining,
a dry wind, acrid with remembering.

At night, stars smudge through a veil of grey particulate
above remains of mansions, trailer parks,
as politicians pour incendiary blame

like gasoline over a landscape,
once pines and peonies, now streaked
with dust of mustard-weed.

Beside the pools where shells once glittered,
the tide has flung a net across the sand—

strewn ash, burnt shards of fence and shingle,
charred bark shavings curled in foam-speckled strands,
a necklace draped over the shore's freckled breast.

Plovers whistle along the beach, searching
for insects and worms inside the shallow footprints
of a single snowy egret, who strides across the litter

toward a sanctuary of sparse foliage,
fragile remnant of life once nourished
by an abundant sea.

Pause

At the top of the elm, still green,
a single leaf shines canary-yellow,
not the subdued topaz we're accustomed to.

September now, and the long-awaited
burnt-sienna, subtle rusts and oranges,
are nowhere in sight. The tenacious earth

clings to its pastels, its primaries—
purple hosta and salvia, red geraniums,
giant rose hibiscus radiating against lawns.

Remember how we children once celebrated
the autumn smoke, squawk of departing geese,
the first few flakes?

This September stands still, looking back
at the crazed summer of isolation, reluctant
to submit to the shrinking light, pausing

one more time to gather-in the sun's warmth,
the flamboyant out-of-doors,
where we've escaped our confinement,

pushing our cramped bodies
into the exuberance swirling over the earth
and into our desperate lungs.

Messages

Stars plummet
through space,
trace their earth-
bound journeys
with fiery plumes,
embers sputter
then fade,
papering lawns
beneath elms
with yellowed leaves,
color of old telegrams,
bits of warmth
for a planet
turned cold, as if

an unexpected wind
had scattered
wrinkled messages
to be collected
and re-read,
pressed and pasted,
stored for a moment
in the ashy-beige
of memory,
pale reminders—
not even stars
are forever.

Black Ice

At three below, our breath
collects the color blue,

the path turns white
with lace adrift on earth, hard-frozen.

Beneath our boots, remnants of past seasons—
scatterings of yellowed leaves, twisted vines,

spinners and petals torn in random patterns—
impaled at the edges of a dark mirror,

resplendent as the night sky, spangled
with lights and transparencies,

altered perceptions, black holes,
the treachery of foothold exposed.

Dizzy with uncertainty, we hold
each other's elbows, lurch side to side,

panting through pursed lips,
patchy faces raw with resolve.

And lest we lose our footing,
a cold wind warns us:

step lightly, travelers,
measure your pace.

Yigdal

The snowy construction site
across the street
contains the shadow of the former
hospital imploded last month,
along with its births and deaths
and heartbreaks, as architects
try to merge what was and is
with what will be.

The ancient elm
outside my ice-feathered sill,
once a lavish summer aviary,
seems dead now, grey with frost,
while a film of mossy green
grazes its northern bark,
quickens its pulse,
warming one season into the next.

O sing praise for this timeless world,
where trees forever host
construction sites for nesting robins.

Alleluia

I thought I heard a phoebe this morning
but it was only wind, and this March sky
is the color of sullen, the sun, dull as a nickel,
and my throat still scratchy from the radiators' dry heat.

So I heave on my old Lands-End long-coat,
(several tons of "ethically-procured down")
grab the worn-out gloves, the wool hat, the Uggs,
and begin my solitary walk in the neighborhood,

where I'm dazzled by a procession of bare-limbed elms
wearing white lace mantillas as they sashay
down Lafayette Avenue, no doubt on their way
to a fancy-dress party on Elmwood, accompanied

by The Oratorio Society of Robins and Cardinals,
who warble soprano arias from Figaro,
and practice Mozart's "Alleluia, Jubilate" in 4 parts,
a fitting anthem for the opening festivities.

At my feet, where snow once obliterated the garden,
snowdrops straighten their bent necks through the mud
and look around at a lightening sky.
And from the dark hedge at the corner—

Listen. Is it a fountain? Yes, an audible spray,

bubbles gushing from a thousand tiny throats,
cascading through the melting silence.

Traces

The glass ledges
overhanging the sidewalk
have disappeared,

uncovering imprints of leaves,
snow-pressed into patterns on pavement,

fringes of last summer's
shriveled salvia mingled

with pinches of dried hydrangea
blown from hollow stems,
traces of what might be coming.

In my wanderings
I heard first what I couldn't see—

squawk and flap above branches—
bravado kept in winter storage, released—

wingspan shadows ruffling
a carpet of purple crocuses
unfurled beneath a locust tree,

its shingled bark speckled
with yellow-green moss,

florescence tossed
across an open path.

Saturday Farmers' Market

In the distance from any direction,
white canvas tents, sails luffed
against a blue dotted-swiss sky,

flaps and table-coverings
ballooned with an exhalation
barely perceptible on the skin,

filled with yapping of dogs,
squeals of liberated children
scrambling among men and women

who weave across tufted lawns,
couples unhurried, arms linked,
faces lit by reflections bouncing off

stacks of satiny blue-black eggplants,
fevered tomatoes, silk-tasseled corn
ready for grilling, ruffled parsley
nestled among baskets of peaches,

and slung from shoulders, burlap sacks
swollen with ingredients for brinjal curry,
corn chowder, fruit tart,

shoppers navigating the stalls,
consumed by the prospect
of creating exotic cuisines in kitchens,

shooting the breeze through their masks
about the weather, news of the neighborhood,
politics and contagion almost forgotten,

reassured by the solidity of earth under sandals,
the breath of shade trees,
the heft of this day's bounty.

The Short Life of the Magnolia

Where yesterday, milky-suede blossoms
blushed from swollen buds
vibrating in an early Spring breeze,

today, curls of bruise-brown petals
litter a greening lawn, as if some god
had demanded a cruel sacrifice,

in exchange for the more subtle gifts of May,
like those unassuming elm leaves
now unfolding on winter-bared branches.

Victim of nature's blind injustice,
magnolia's emergent bounty,
like first desire,

sets itself aflame soon after it appears,
its ardor self-consuming, too celebrated,
too exquisite to remain.

Summer Day

Let's sit here on the screened porch
near the bird-feeder
overlooking a sea of wild-flowers,

inhale the breath of honeysuckle,
purple yarrow, belled foxglove,

watch the languid bees
hovering over each delicious blossom
doing their life's work.

But don't nod off just yet,
drowsy with contentment.

If we wait, the birds will come,
startling in their finery,

goldfinches and cardinals
chattering like children,
vying for a few seeds and suet,

pileated woodpeckers
chasing them into the air—

yellow and crimson arcs
splashed across a cornflower field.

Their songs will lift us,
quicken our winter hearts.
Wait for them.

This is Susan Dworski Nusbaum's fourth poetry collection. Her books, *What We Take With Us*, *Open Wide, the Eye*, and *Alive in This Place*, were released by Coffeetown Press in 2014, 2016, and 2019.

Born in Rochester, NY, she received a BA from Smith College and a law degree from the University of Buffalo Law School. She lives in Buffalo NY where she raised her family, and worked as a musician, teacher, arts administrator, and most recently as an attorney.

Her work has appeared in numerous publications, including *The Connecticut River Review*, *Poetry East*, *Woven Tale Press*, *Nimrod International Journal*, *Chautauqua Literary Journal*, *Calliope*, *Chautauqua*, *Harpur Palate*, *Wisconsin Review*, *The Sow's Ear*, *A Celebration of Western New York Poets*, (2014), *The Buffalo News*.

She has presented her poems in solo public readings in several communities in the Northeast and Florida.

www.ingramcontent.com/pod-product-compliance
Lightning Source LLC
Chambersburg PA
CBHW060617080526
44585CB00013B/867